Bats

by Joelle Riley

Lerner Publications Company • Minneapolis

To the Batty-Bats: Teri, Leandra, and Kiran

Photos are reproduced with the permission of the following sources: all photos © Merlin D. Tuttle, Bat Conservation International, except p. 4, © Joe McDonald/Visuals Unlimited; p. 23, © Joe McDonald/CORBIS; p. 24, © Wendy Dennis/Visuals Unlimited; p. 26, © Elaine Acker, Bat Conservation International; p. 41, © Dan Taylor, Bat Conservation International; pp. 46–47, © Karen Marks, Bat Conservation International; cover, © Joe McDonald/CORBIS.

Lerner Publications Company
A division of Lerner Publishing Group
241 First Avenue North
Minneapolis, Minnesota 55401 U.S.A.

Website address: www.lernerbooks.com

Library of Congress Cataloging-in-Publication Data

    Bats / by Joelle Riley
      p.   cm. — (Early bird nature books)
    Includes index.
    ISBN: 0–8225–2416–3 (lib. bdg. : alk. paper)
    1. Bats—Juvenile literature. I. Title. II. Series.
  QL737.C5R493 2005
  599.4—dc22   2004007416

Manufactured in the United States of America
1 2 3 4 5 6 – JR – 10 09 08 07 06 05

Contents

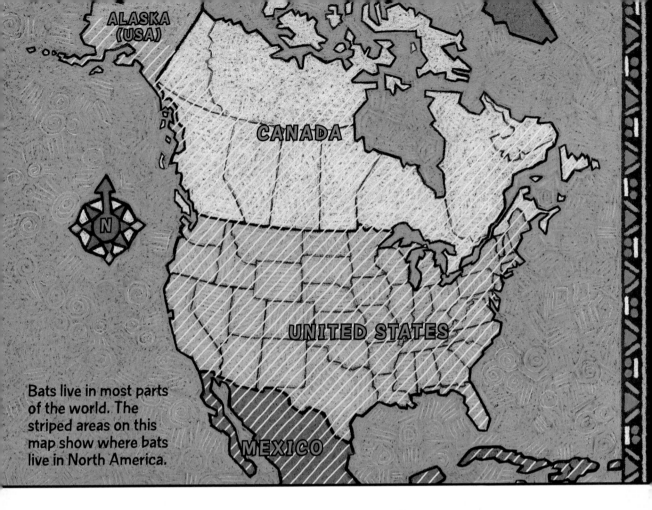

ALASKA (USA)

CANADA

N

UNITED STATES

Bats live in most parts of the world. The striped areas on this map show where bats live in North America.

MEXICO

Be a Word Detective

Can you find these words as you read about the bat's life?
Be a detective and try to figure out what they mean.
You can turn to the glossary on page 46 for help.

colony	hibernate	nocturnal
echolocation	hover	predators
endangered	mammals	prey
habitats	migrating	roosts

5

These bats are flying out of a cave at sunset. All bats have wings and fly to get around. Are bats a type of bird?

Night Flyers

The sun goes down. The sky gets dark. Small shapes begin to dart around in the air. The shapes are bats.

Bats and birds both fly. But bats are not birds. Bats belong to the group of animals called mammals. Bats, mice, dogs, and people are all mammals. Female mammals feed their babies milk from their bodies. And all mammals have hair.

This baby bat is staying close to its mother. They are fruit bats from Africa.

Bats have soft, silky hair called fur. A bat's fur is usually black, brown, or gray. But some bats have red, yellow, or white fur. And some bats have spots or stripes of different colors.

This hoary bat has thick fur. A bat cleans its fur by licking it, just as a cat does.

Some kinds of bats can hover. Hovering bats often have short, wide wings.

Bats are the only mammals that can fly. Many kinds of bats can turn and twist quickly in the air. Some kinds can even hover (HUH-vuhr). Hovering is staying still in one place in the air. Bats hover by flapping their wings very quickly.

A bat's wings have no hair. The wings are made of thin skin stretched over the bat's arm, hand, and leg bones. A bat's wings are so thin that light can shine through them. But they are also very strong. A bat has powerful chest muscles. These muscles make the bat's wings flap.

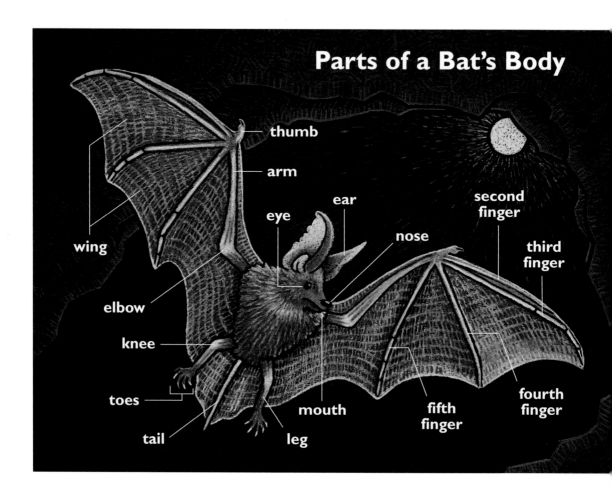

Parts of a Bat's Body

thumb

arm

ear

eye

nose

second finger

wing

third finger

elbow

knee

toes

fourth finger

mouth

fifth finger

tail

leg

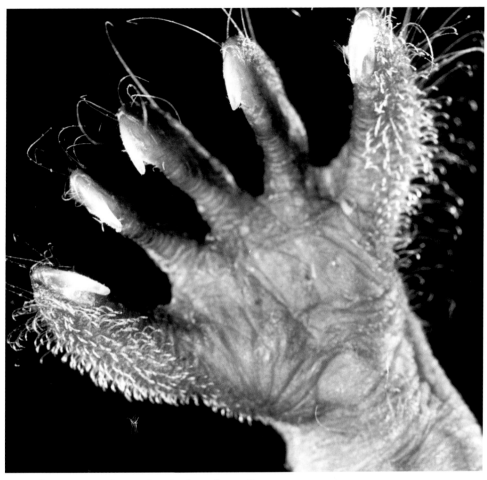

Bats have two feet. Each foot has five toes.

A bat's feet are strong too. When the bat rests, it hangs by its feet. On each toe is a claw. A bat's claws can hold on to almost anything. The bat can hang from a tree branch or from the ceiling of a cave.

Most bats can't walk very well. They can only crawl a bit on their legs and folded wings. The only bats that can move well on the ground are the vampire bats. These bats have strong legs. Vampire bats can hop like frogs. They can even hop into the air and fly away.

Vampire bats can walk, run, hop, and jump.
They have very strong legs.

But most bats can't start flying from the ground. They need to take off from a high place, such as the branch of a tree. If a bat is on the ground, it has to climb up a tree or a rock so that it can fly. Bats have tiny claws on their wings. They use these claws to climb.

This bat is using its claws to climb along a tree branch. Bats have special leg muscles to open and close their claws.

To fly, a bat lets go of the branch or rock it is hanging from. It falls for just a moment. Then the bat starts flapping its wings. Flapping makes the bat stop falling and start flying.

A pallid bat flaps its wings as it starts to fly. A bat's strong shoulder muscles help it fly.

This bat eats ripe fruit. It uses its teeth to mash up the fruit. Then it licks the sticky juice from its face.

Bats have bright little eyes. A bat's mouth is full of sharp little teeth. A bat's ears may be tiny, or they may be bigger than the bat's head!

Flying fox bats (above) *have a long nose and small, doglike ears. Australian ghost bats* (inset) *have a flap of skin on their noses and rabbitlike ears.*

Scientists have found more than 1,100 different species, or kinds, of bats. They belong to two main groups. The first group is the large bats. A large bat's face looks much like the face of a dog or a fox. So some people call these bats flying foxes. The other group is the small bats. Some small bats have extra flaps of skin on their noses or in front of their ears. These bats' faces can look very strange.

The biggest bat in the world is called the gigantic flying fox. Its wings measure up to 6 feet from tip to tip. That's longer than a bicycle! The smallest bat in the world is the bumblebee bat. This tiny bat's wings are only about 6 inches across. It weighs less than a penny weighs.

The gigantic flying fox (above) is the largest type of bat. It lives in Africa, Asia, and Australia. The bumblebee bat (inset) is the smallest mammal in the world. It lives in Thailand, a country in Asia.

Chapter 2

A lesser long-nosed bat feeds from the fruit of a cactus. What else do bats eat?

Finding Food

Bats are nocturnal. Nocturnal animals look for food at night. Different kinds of bats eat different kinds of food.

Large bats eat only plant foods. Some large bats eat fruit. These bats are sometimes called fruit bats. Other large bats drink nectar. Nectar is a sweet liquid that flowers make. These bats also eat pollen. Pollen is a yellow powder inside flowers. Flowers use pollen to make seeds. A large bat uses its eyes and its nose to find fruit or flowers.

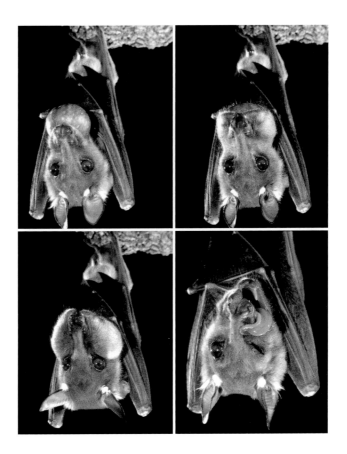

This bat is eating a fruit called a fig. A bat can eat very quickly. It will spit out any part of the fruit it can't chew.

Small bats are predators (PREH-duh-turz).
Predators are animals that hunt other animals.
The animals that small bats hunt are called
their prey.

This pallid bat has caught a scorpion. Scorpions have stingers that can hurt many kinds of animals. But scorpions can't hurt pallid bats.

Some bats swoop low over lakes or ponds. They listen for the ripples fish make as they swim. When the bats hear a fish, they snatch it out of the water and carry it away to eat it.

Most small bats eat insects such as moths and mosquitoes. Some eat larger animals, such as scorpions, centipedes, lizards, birds, mice, and even small fish. Vampire bats drink the blood of animals such as cattle and birds.

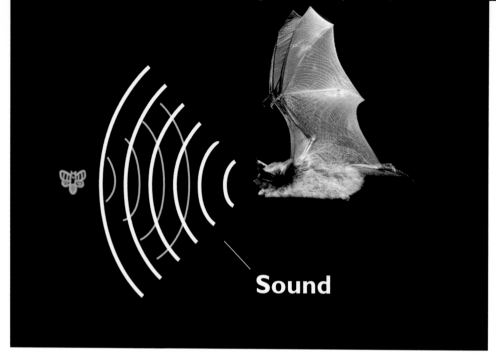

Sound

Many bats use echolocation to find flying insects at night.

Small bats use their sense of hearing to find food. The way small bats find their food is called echolocation (EHK-oh-loh-KAY-shuhn). To use echolocation, a bat makes many tiny noises. The noises are so high-pitched that people can't hear them. But the bat can hear these sounds. The sounds hit objects like the ground, tree branches, and insects. Then the sounds echo back to the bat. The bat hears the echoes and knows where to fly to catch its prey.

Bats also use echolocation to keep from bumping into objects as they fly. Even when there is no light, a bat can fly fast without running into tree branches.

This little brown bat uses echolocation to fly around branches.

Chapter 3

Hanging high above the ground keeps bats safe from enemies. Where do bats rest?

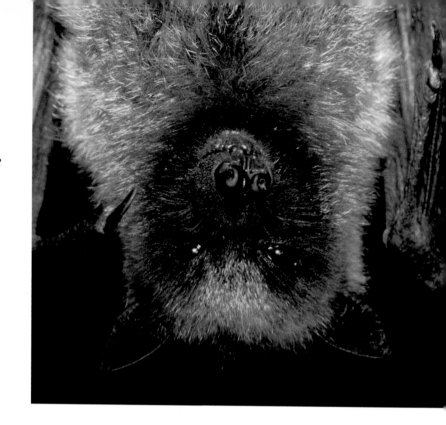

Bat Homes

Bats live in most parts of the world. They live in forests. They live in grassy places that have only a few trees. They even live in hot deserts. But no bats live near the North Pole or the South Pole. These places are too cold for bats.

The places where bats can live are called their habitats (HAB-uh-tats). A bat's habitat has to have three things. It has to have food to eat, water to drink, and safe places to rest. Bats' resting places are called roosts.

When bats rest, it is called roosting. These bats are roosting in a cave.

Some bats live alone. But some bats share their roosts with other bats. A group of bats living together is called a colony. Some colonies have thousands or millions of bats!

Bracken Cave near San Antonio, Texas, is the largest bat colony in the world. Twenty million bats live there.

Bats roost in this old iron mine. But the mine is in a place that has cold winters. Bats can't find food when it's cold outside.

Some bat habitats never get very cold. Bats can find food in these places all year long. But other places have cold winters. When it is cold, bats can't find food to eat. And if it gets very cold, bats can freeze.

This bat is hibernating. The bat's body has cooled down so much that cold drops of water cover its fur.

Some bats hibernate (HY-buhr-nayt) when winter comes. When a bat hibernates, it goes into a kind of deep sleep that lasts for a long time. Its heartbeat and breathing become very slow. Its body cools down. Many bats hibernate in caves. The cave must be quiet and safe. It must be cold. But it can't be so cold that the bat will freeze.

Some bats fly to warmer places when winter comes. Traveling when the seasons change is called migrating. Some bats migrate to places where they can find plenty of food all winter long. Others migrate to places where they can hibernate until spring comes.

Some bats migrate to find a warm place to spend the winter. In summer, they return home. Bats that live in caves usually return to the same cave every year.

Chapter 4

This Mexican free-tailed bat is snuggling with its baby. How many babies do most bats have at one time?

Baby Bats

Baby bats are called pups. Most mother bats have one pup each year.

When a bat pup is born, it can't fly. All it can do is hold on to things and drink its mother's milk. When a pup drinks milk, it snuggles under its mother's wing.

Milk from its mother will help this pup grow fast. A pup nurses at least twice a day.

Mother bats can find their own pups even in very crowded roosts. A mother bat knows the sound of her pup's voice. A mother also knows how her pup smells.

Some kinds of bats carry their pups with them all the time. The pups use their claws to hold tightly to their mother's fur. They hang on even while she hunts for food. They stay with their mother until they learn to fly.

Other kinds of bats have special roosts where pups are born. These roosts are called nursery roosts. Nursery roosts are usually in caves.

A nursery roost may be used by just a few mother bats. But some nursery roosts are used by thousands of bats. When a pup is born, its mother helps it grab onto the ceiling of the cave. The baby huddles together with many other pups. The pups keep each other warm while their mothers hunt for food.

Pups have strong legs and claws to hang on to their mother or their roost.

Bat pups grow very quickly. They learn to fly by the time they are about one month old. Soon after that, they learn how to find their own food. Then the pups leave the nursery roost.

A flying fox feeds on the nectar of a coral tree. Many bats are born in the spring and summer when there are plenty of insects, fruit, and flowers to eat.

Little brown bats can live to be 30 years old.

Bats live much longer than most small mammals. Mice live no more than 2 or 3 years. But many bats live to be more than 20 years old.

Chapter 5

These flying fox bats hang in a tree far away from people's homes. But some bats live near people. Why would bats come close to houses and towns?

People and Bats

For a very long time, people have told stories about bats. Many people think bats are scary or dangerous. This is not true. Bats are very shy. They want to stay away from people.

But people's towns can be good places for bats to live. The attics and porch roofs of some houses make good roosts. And it's easy for bats to find food in towns, because swarms of insects gather around streetlights.

Little brown bats fly around an old church. Spaces under roofs can make good roosts. Some bats also roost under bridges.

Sometimes bats cause problems for people. Big colonies of bats are noisy and smelly. And sometimes bats get sick. If a person touches a sick bat, the person may get sick too.

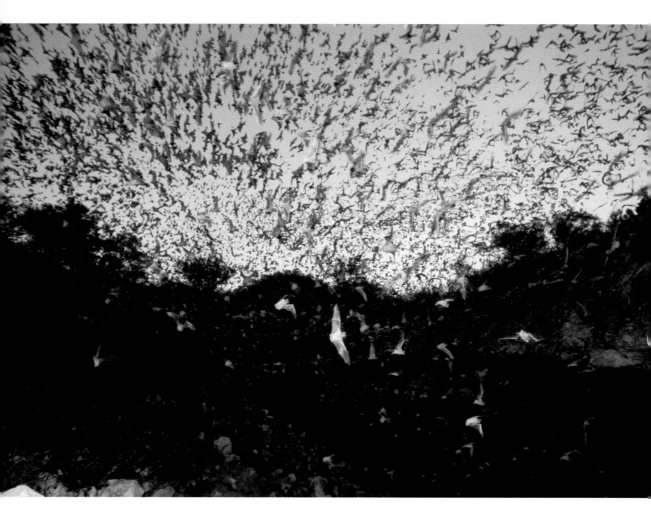

Large groups of flying bats scare some people. But bats are gentle animals. They do not attack people.

Sometimes trees are cut down and burned to make room for farms or houses. Bats that lived in those trees must find new places to roost.

People cause problems for bats too. Some people kill bats because they are afraid of them. And people destroy bat habitat. When people cut down forests or cover the entrances to caves, they destroy bats' homes.

Many kinds of bats are endangered. That means they are in danger of dying out forever. Some may already have died out.

The lesser long-nosed bat is one kind of bat that is endangered. It lives in the southwestern United States and Mexico.

This scientist is putting a radio tag on a myotis bat. Scientists track radio signals to learn where bats live, feed, and migrate.

Scientists are studying bats to learn more about them. The scientists catch bats and put tiny radio tags on them. Then they let the bats go. The tags send radio signals that tell scientists where the bats fly. Scientists also use special machines to hear the sounds bats make as they use echolocation. We have learned a lot about some bats. But there is still much more that we don't know.

The plants on which bananas, avocados, and other fruits grow live in places where there are many fruit bats. The bats carry these plants' seeds and orphan pollen.

Bats are important animals. Large bats help plants to grow. When a bat eats fruit, it eats the seeds too. It carries the seeds to new places where they can grow. When a bat eats nectar from a flower, pollen sticks to its fur. When the bat visits a different flower, some of the pollen rubs off. The second flower uses the pollen to make seeds that will grow into new plants.

People watch Mexican free-tailed bats come out of their cave at night. Some caves attract many visitors who want to learn more about bats.

Bats that eat insects help to control the number of insects in the world. A little brown bat can catch and eat 1,200 mosquitoes in just one hour!

The next time you're outside just after sunset, look for bats in the sky. Watch them as they dart after moths and mosquitoes. And think how many bug bites you'd get if there were no bats!

On Sharing a Book

As you know, adults greatly influence a child's attitude toward reading. When a child sees you read, or when you share a book with a child, you're sending a message that reading is important. Show the child that reading a book together is important to you. Find a comfortable, quiet place. Turn off the television and limit other distractions, such as telephone calls.

Be prepared to start slowly. Take turns reading parts of this book. Stop and talk about what you're reading. Talk about the photographs. You may find that much of the shared time is spent discussing just a few pages. This discussion time is valuable for both of you, so don't move through the book too quickly. If the child begins to lose interest, stop reading. Continue sharing the book at another time. When you do pick up the book again, be sure to revisit the parts you have already read. Most importantly, enjoy the book!

Be a Vocabulary Detective

You will find a word list on page 5. Words selected for this list are important to the understanding of the topic of this book. Encourage the child to be a word detective and search for the words as you read the book together. Talk about what the words mean and how they are used in the sentence. Do any of these words have more than one meaning? You will find these words defined in a glossary on page 46.

What about Questions?

Use questions to make sure the child understands the information in this book. Here are some suggestions:

> What did this paragraph tell us? What does this picture show? What do you think we'll learn about next? How are bats like other mammals? How are they different? What do bats eat? Could a bat live in your backyard? Why/Why not? What are baby bats called? How long does a young bat live with its mother? How do people cause problems for bats? What do you think it's like being a bat? What is your favorite part of the book? Why?

If the child has questions, don't hesitate to respond with questions of your own, such as What do *you* think? Why? What is it that you don't know? If the child can't remember certain facts, turn to the index.

Introducing the Index

The index is an important learning tool. It helps readers get information quickly without searching throughout the whole book. Turn to the index on page 47. Choose an entry, such as *homes,* and ask the child to use the index to find out where bats live. Repeat this exercise with as many entries as you like. Ask the child to point out the differences between an index and a glossary. (The index helps readers find information quickly, while the glossary tells readers what words mean.)

Where in the World?

Many plants and animals found in the Early Bird Nature Books series live in parts of the world other than the United States. Encourage the child to find the places mentioned in this book on a world map or globe. Take time to talk about climate, terrain, and how you might live in such places.

All the World in Metric!

Although our monetary system is in metric units (based on multiples of 10), the United States is one of the few countries in the world that does not use the metric system of measurement. Here are some conversion activities you and the child can do using a calculator:

WHEN YOU KNOW:	MULTIPLY BY:	TO FIND:
miles	1.609	kilometers
feet	0.3048	meters
inches	2.54	centimeters
gallons	3.785	liters
tons	0.907	metric tons
pounds	0.454	kilograms

Activities

Go to the library or visit websites to learn more about bats. The bat website run by Bat Conservation International (http://www.batcon.org) is a good place to start.

Pretend to be a bat. How do you walk? How do you eat? What sounds do you make?

Make up a story about bats. Be sure to include information from this book. Draw or paint pictures to illustrate your story.

Glossary

colony: a group of animals living together

echolocation (EHK-oh-loh-KAY-shuhn): a way of finding something by sending out a sound and listening for its echo. Bats use echolocation to find their way in the dark.

endangered: in danger of dying out forever

habitats (HAB-uh-tats): areas where a kind of animal can live and grow

hibernate (HY-buhr-nayt): to go into a kind of deep sleep for a long time. Some bats hibernate during cold weather, when food is hard to find.

hover (HUH-vuhr): to stay in one place in the air

mammals: animals that have hair and feed their babies milk from their bodies

migrating: traveling to another area to live when the seasons change

nocturnal: active at night

predators (PREH-duh-turz): animals that hunt and eat other animals

prey: animals that are hunted and eaten by other animals

roosts: safe places for bats to rest

Index

Pages listed in **bold** type refer to photographs.

About the Author

Joelle Riley is an author and editor of children's books. She lives in Minneapolis, Minnesota, with her two greyhounds and two cats. Her books for Lerner Publishing Group include *Buzzing Bumblebees, Pouncing Bobcats, Quiet Owls,* and *The Nervous System.*